SOCCER ICONS

MESSI

WELBECK
CHILDREN'S BOOKS

First published in the USA in 2026 by
Welbeck Children's Books
An imprint of Hachette Children's Group
Part of Hodder & Stoughton Limited
Carmelite House, 50 Victoria Embankment
London EC4Y 0DZ

DISCLAIMER
All trademarks, brands, company names, team names, registered names, individual names, products, logos and catchphrases used or cited in this book are the property of their respective owners and used in this book for informational and identifying purposes only. This book is a publication of Welbeck Children's Books and has not been licensed, approved, sponsored or endorsed by any person or entity.

MIX
Paper | Supporting responsible forestry
FSC® C104740
www.fsc.org

ISBN 978 1 83955 364 6
1 3 5 7 9 10 8 6 4 2
Printed in China

An Hachette UK Company
www.hachette.co.uk
www.hachettechildrens.co.uk

The website addresses (URLs) included in this book were valid at the time of going to press. However, it is possible that contents or addresses may have changed since the publication of this book. No responsibility for any such changes can be accepted by either the author or the publisher.

All facts and stats correct as of May 2026

SOCCER ICONS

MESSI

CONTENTS

adidas
AFA
10
AFA

HELLO LEO!

Welcome to the ultimate guide for young fans who want to know everything about Lionel Messi. Packed with fun facts, stats, and amazing records, it celebrates one of soccer's greatest-ever stars.

Messi is the incredible **Argentine forward** who set the standard for the modern soccer player. Starting out as a kid with big dreams at **Barcelona's La Masia** academy, the world was soon watching his **dribbling**, **clever passes**, and **unbelievable goals**.

Messi shows what happens when **talent** meets **hard work**. For more than **twenty years**, he has amazed fans with his **creativity** and love for soccer. Today, he is a **hero** to millions of young players around the world.

Read on to discover Messi's most **exciting matches**, **coolest goals** and huge collection of **trophies**. At the end of the book, try the **quiz** to see how much you know about the incredible player known as 'Leo'.

TURN THE PAGE TO KICK THINGS OFF!

RAISED IN ROSARIO

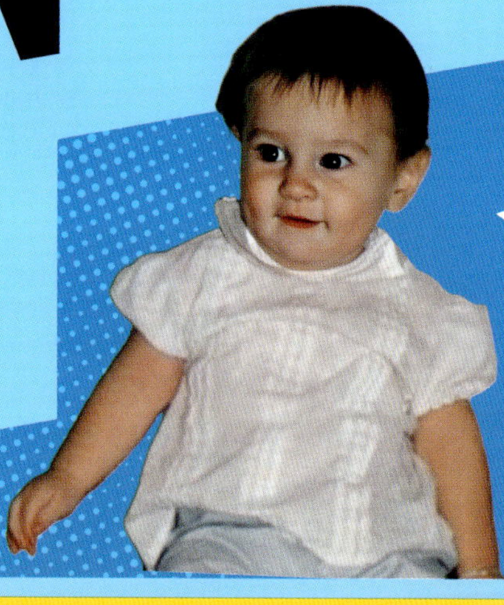

Messi grew up in **Rosario**, a busy city in Argentina, where he was the third of four children. His family didn't have a lot of money, but they had plenty of love. Messi and his family shared **one big passion—soccer**. Leo was always outside playing soccer with his brothers and cousins. Even with a worn-out ball, his **quick feet** and **clever tricks** soon made him the best player on the block.

1987

Lionel Andrés Messi is born on **June 24**. His parents Jorge and Celia are both factory workers.

1991

Little Leo starts playing for his local team, **Grandoli**.

1994

At the age of seven, Messi joins the youth team at his first professional club, **Newell's Old Boys**.

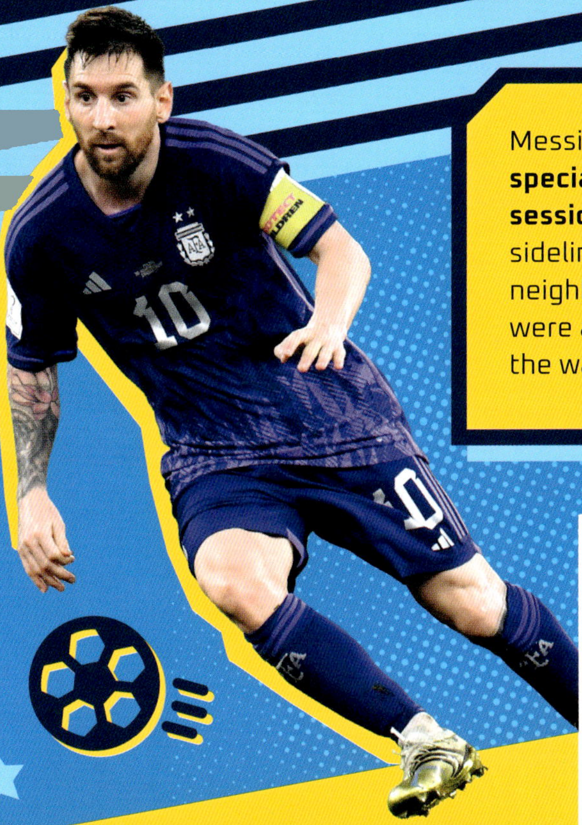

Messi's grandmother, Celia, noticed how **special** Leo was. She often took him to **training sessions** and **games**, cheering loudly from the sidelines. When **Messi was four**, he joined his neighbourhood club, **Grandoli**. The coaches were amazed by his **balance**, **close control**, and the way he could **beat players** twice his size.

"MY FIRST MEMORIES ARE FROM WHEN I WAS VERY LITTLE, MAYBE THREE OR FOUR YEARS OLD PLAYING IN MY NEIGHBOURHOOD AT HOME. I CAN PICTURE MYSELF WITH THE BALL AT MY FEET FROM A VERY YOUNG AGE."

– **Lionel Messi**

2001

Messi and his family move to **Spain**, where the 13-year-old joins the academy at **Barcelona**.

NEWELL'S YOUNG BOY

After Grandoli, Leo moved across town to join the youth team at **Newell's Old Boys**, a famous club in Rosario. For the first few years he played **seven-a-side** games in a team of boys born in 1987. They became known as the **Machine of 87** and were virtually unbeatable as they progressed to full eleven-a-side matches.

2004

Messi makes his **La Liga** debut for Barcelona, at age just 17.

2005

Wins La Liga in his **debut season**—it was Barcelona's first title since 1999.

2009

Messi wins a historic **treble** of La Liga, Copa del Rey, and the Champions League, followed by his first **Ballon d'Or**.

A growth condition meant Leo was much smaller than most of the other boys, but that helped his **balance**, **dribbling**, and **close control**. Little Messi could beat players with ease and it was obvious early on that he was special. But as Leo got older, his size would become a problem without treatment.

Everything changed for Leo in 2000, when he travelled to Spain for a trial at **Barcelona**. The club invited him to join **La Masia** and offered to help with the treatment he needed. So, **at age 13**, Messi left Argentina to start a new life in Barcelona. His dad Jorge moved with him, but being away from the rest of his family and friends was difficult. Leo overcame his homesickness by focusing on soccer.

2011

In a record-breaking **53-goal season**, Messi helps Barcelona to the La Liga and Champions League double.

2012

He becomes the first player to win the Ballon d'Or for a **fourth** time.

STAR SHOT

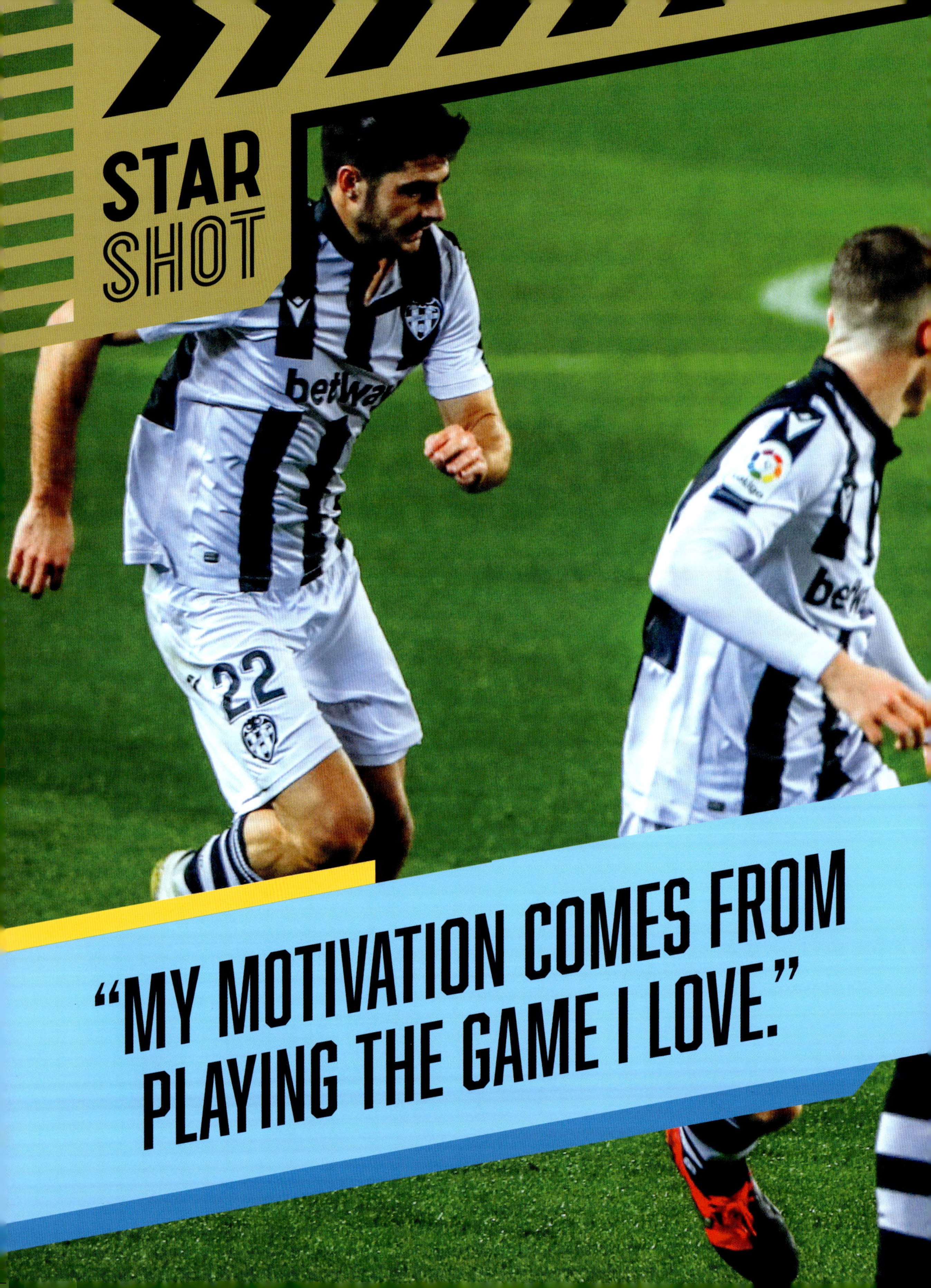

"MY MOTIVATION COMES FROM PLAYING THE GAME I LOVE."

Rakuten

SEVEN MEGA MESSI FACTS

1

Messi was named Lionel after the famous singer **Lionel Richie**, whose music his parents loved.

2

At Newell's Old Boys, Messi often wore the **number 10** shirt—a number he would later wear with distinction for club and country.

3

Messi is said to have scored **500 goals** for the Machine of 87 team at Newell's Old Boys.

4

His original contract with Barcelona was signed on a **napkin** in a restaurant.

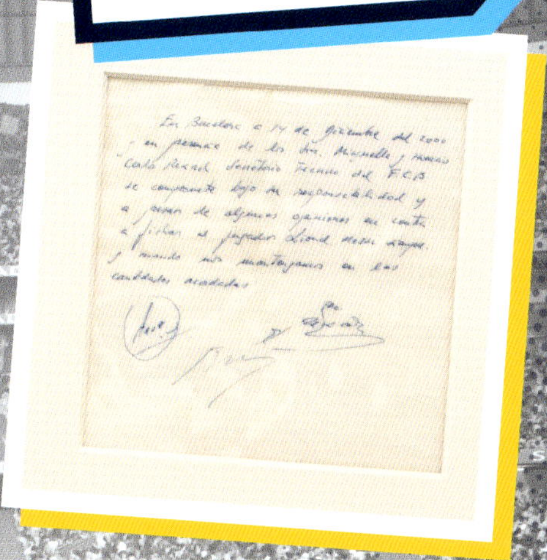

5

Messi's **goal celebration** of pointing both hands to the sky is in tribute to his late grandmother.

6

When Messi was **17**, he trained with **Barcelona's first team** for the first time. The senior players couldn't believe how good he was.

7

At La Masia, his team-mates nicknamed Leo **"The Flea."**

ONLINE LEO

Messi is famously quiet and humble, but social media lets him share moments from his life with fans around the world. To celebrate his biggest achievements and follow his journey, here's where to find Leo online...

INSTAGRAM

@leomessi

511 million+ followers

FACEBOOK

facebook.com/leomessi

116 million+ followers

You can also keep up to date with Messi's national side on the Argentina FA official channels:

INSTAGRAM: @AFAseleccion
X: @Argentina

STAR SHOT

"EVERYTHING I DID, I DID FOR FOOTBALL, TO ACHIEVE MY DREAM."

BARCELONA BREAKTHROUGH

Messi made his first team debut for Barcelona in 2004 at just 17. He quickly caught everyone's attention with his speed and dribbling skills. Barca fans loved watching him glide past defenders as if the ball was tied to his cleats.

When Leo broke into the Barcelona first team, the club's biggest star was the Brazilian ace **Ronaldinho**. He helped Leo settle in and treated him like his **little brother.** He even provided the assist for Messi's **first goal** for Barcelona!

2015

Messi wins the **treble** for a second time with Barcelona.

2021

Makes a sensational move to France, to join **Paris Saint-Germain**.

2022

Messi fulfills his dream to lift the **World Cup** with Argentina in Qatar.

In the 2006-07 season, Messi began to put in the kind of **performances** that would make him a star. In March 2007, he scored the first **El Clasico hat-trick** in 12 years when he **equalized three times** against Real Madrid.

Messi inherited the iconic number 10 shirt from Ronaldinho.

2023

Moves to the **USA** to play soccer for the MLS side **Inter Miami**.

PLAYING FOR PEP

In 2008, Pep Guardiola became Barcelona manager. His team, built around Messi and midfielders such as Xavi and Andrés Iniesta, played fast, attacking soccer with lots of possession and clever passing—it became known as "tiki taka." With Messi leading the way, Barcelona became unstoppable!

In the 2008-09 season, Messi helped Barcelona win **La Liga**, the **Copa del Rey**, and the **Champions League** all in the same year.

In the Champions League final against Manchester United, Messi scored a famous header to secure the 2-0 win.

The following season (2009-10) Messi ended the year with **34 league goals**, winning the **Golden Boot** as the top scorer in Spain and the European Golden Shoe. He was **top scorer (8 goals)** in the Champions League, too.

BARCELONA FAST FACTS

Here are seven brilliant Barcelona facts every Messi fan should know...

1

In 2009, Messi helped Barcelona win the sextuple—**six major trophies** in one year.

2

Messi scored the **first goal** of the Pep Guardiola era in a **La Liga** match against Racing Santander.

3

In 2009, Messi won his first **Ballon d'Or** at the age of just **22**.

4

In 2010, Messi became the first Barcelona player in the modern era to score **back-to-back league hat-tricks** since the 1940s.

5

By the end of the 2011-12 season, Messi had become **Barcelona's all-time top scorer**.

6

Messi scored Barcelona's **5,000th goal** in the league in 2009.

7

Messi became the first player to **score five goals** in a Champions League match against Bayer Leverkusen in 2012.

TEAM PERFECTION

By the 2010–11 season, Barcelona was playing some of the best soccer in the world, and Messi was at its heart. A La Liga and Champions League double, with Messi the top scorer in Europe, capped an outstanding season.

Messi was **unstoppable** in the 2010-11 Champions League. A brilliant **solo goal** against Real Madrid in the semi-final was followed by **another cool finish** in the final, where Manchester United was beaten again.

Throughout 2011–12, Messi scored at an unbelievable rate, breaking record after record. He ended the season with **73 goals** in all competitions—the most scored by a player in a **single European season**. It was one of soccer's greatest individual seasons.

In 2012, Messi became the first player to win the Ballon d'Or four times—and in consecutive years.

FAME AND FORTUNE

Messi is one of the world's most admired athletes. From his early days at Barcelona to lifting trophies for club and country, he has become more than a soccer player—he is a global icon known for his skill, humility, and kindness.

Messi is ranked among the world's **highest paid** athletes. Through soccer, **sponsorships**, and long-term **partnerships** with major brands, he has built a huge global profile.

A set of jerseys that Messi wore at the **2022 World Cup** sold at auction in 2023 for **£6.1 million** ($7.8 million).

Messi's **number 10** shirt is recognized everywhere, from the **Americas** to **Asia**.

"I NEVER WANTED TO BE THE BEST. I JUST WANTED TO ENJOY PLAYING FOOTBALL."

– Lionel Messi

In Barcelona, fans visit **murals**, **statues**, and **museums** celebrating his achievements.

Likewise, in the Argentine capital **Buenos Aires**, there are **statues** and **monuments** honouring one of the country's **most famous sports stars**.

HELPING OTHERS

Messi is known for his humility and kindness off the field. He has supported charities since his teens and uses his fame to help children and families around the world.

In 2007, he created the **Leo Messi Foundation**, which helps young people access **education**, **sport**, and **medical care**. The Foundation has helped build and improve **children's hospitals** in Argentina and Spain, including new cancer treatment centers.

During the COVID 19 pandemic, Messi **donated money** to **hospitals** in Barcelona and Rosario to help buy **equipment** and **supplies**.

Messi has supported **youth soccer** in Argentina. He helped fund **Sarmiento**, a club in Rosario, paying for facilities and all-weather fields. Messi has also **mentored players** at Newell's Old Boys and other Argentine teams.

At Newell's Old Boys, Messi helped build a new **gym** and a **dormitory** for academy players in 2012.

LEO'S CARS

Leo is known for being modest on the pitch, but his car collection is anything but humble. His fleet of luxury vehicles and ultra-rare supercars is worth millions and is thought to include...

PAGANI ZONDA TRICOLORE

Zondas are made in very limited numbers and only **three** of this **special Tricolore** edition left the factory—Messi has one of them.

FERRARI 335 SPORT SCAGLIETTI

Messi has been linked with this rare Ferrari. One was sold at auction in 2016 for more than **£25 million ($34 million)**. The buyer wasn't confirmed.

AUDI RS6

When Barcelona partnered with Audi for 10 years, Messi added **three** of them to his garage, including the superfast **RS6 Avant**.

BENTLEY BENTAYGA

Messi can travel in luxury in this **SUV**—a favourite with the **super-rich**.

CADILLAC ESCALADE

After moving to the USA, Leo embraced life in **Miami** by cruising around in an **Escalade**.

THE MSN YEARS

From 2014 to 2017, Messi played alongside Luis Suárez and Neymar. Known as "MSN," they became one of soccer's most formidable attacking trios. Here are seven things you need to know about the MSN years at Barcelona.

1

In their very first season together, **Messi**, **Suárez** and **Neymar** (MSN) scored **122 goals**—the most by a trio in Spanish soccer at the time.

2

MSN led the attack in the **2015 Champions League final** against Juventus, helping Barcelona **win 3-1**.

3

MSN broke their own record in 2015-16, scoring **131 goals.**

5

Between 2014 and 2017, Messi **provided more assists** to Neymar and Suárez than to any other teammates in his career.

4

Against Celta Vigo in 2016, Messi **passed a penalty sideways** for Suárez to score—a sassy moment!

6

In three seasons, MSN helped Barca win **nine trophies**, including **La Liga**, the **Champions League**, and the **FIFA Club World Cup**.

7

The attacking trio combined to score **364 goals** and a record **211 assists** in the three seasons they played together.

FIVE STAR FINISHES

Messi lit up Spanish soccer for nearly two decades. Here are five of his greatest La Liga and Copa del Rey moments for Barcelona.

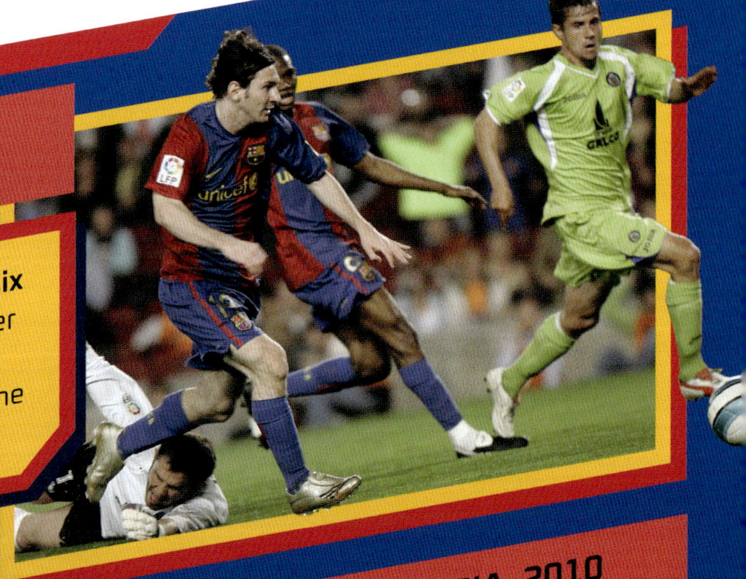

COPA DEL REY SEMI-FINAL VS. GETAFE, 2007

In a stunning **solo run**, Messi beat **six players** and **rounded** the goalkeeper to score a **legendary goal**— often compared to Maradona's "Goal of the Century" at the 1986 World Cup.

LA LIGA VS. VALENCIA, 2010

Messi scored a superb **hat-trick**, including a trademark **curling finish**, showcasing his **unstoppable form** during Barcelona's peak years.

COPA DEL REY VS. MALAGA, 2013

Messi opened the scoring with a brilliant solo move, **weaving through defenders** before firing into the corner.

COPA DEL REY FINAL VS. ATHLETIC BILBAO, 2015

Messi scored one of his **finest goals**, dribbling past **multiple defenders** from the halfway line before finishing at the near post.

COPA DEL REY FINAL VS. SEVILLA, 2016

Messi delivered **two brilliant assists** in extra time, guiding Barcelona to victory in a tense, physical final.

MESSI VERSUS RONALDO

For nine seasons between 2009 and 2018, one of the greatest rivalries in soccer was played out in Spain—Messi versus Cristiano Ronaldo. Here are four El Clásico moments where Messi got the better of his rival at Real Madrid.

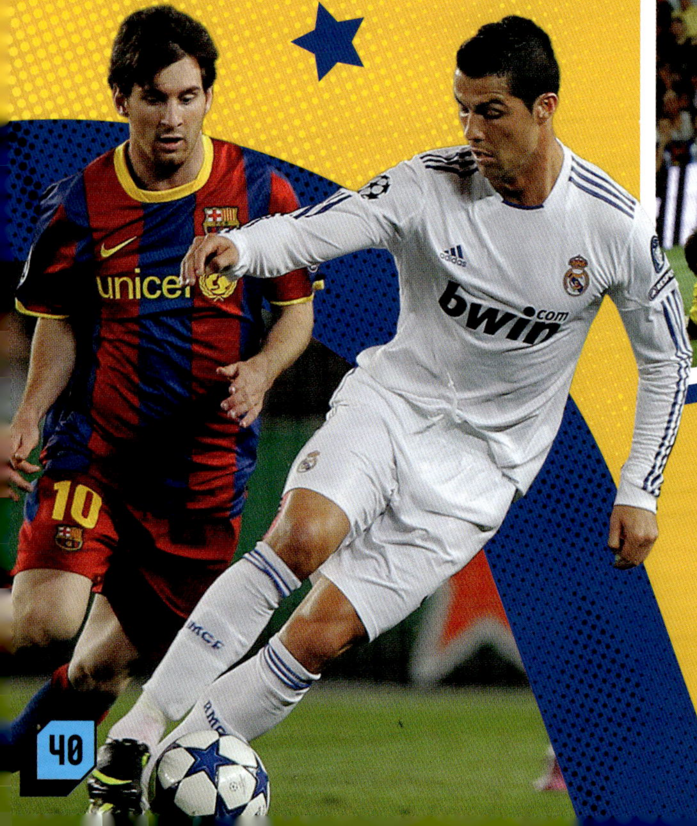

1

In the **Spanish Super Cup** second leg at the Nou Camp in 2011, Messi **scored twice** and assisted another in a **thrilling 3-2 win**.

2

Messi's **two brilliant assists** delivered a 5-0 victory over Real Madrid in La Liga. His **control of the game** helped Barcelona dominate possession and left Ronaldo's side chasing shadows.

3

In a dramatic **El Clásico** at the Bernabéu in 2017, Messi scored a **92nd-minute winner** to secure a 3-2 victory. He celebrated by removing his shirt and holding it up to the Real Madrid fans.

4

During the first leg of the **Champions League** semi-final, Messi scored **both goals** in a 2-0 victory for Barcelona. The second was a **solo effort** that silenced the Bernabéu.

CHAMPIONS LEAGUE MAGIC

Some of the most unforgettable moments in Champions League history came from Messi's time at Barcelona. Here are five of his greatest performances on Europe's biggest stage.

ROUND OF 16 SECOND LEG VS. ARSENAL, 2011

In a career-best display, Messi **scored twice** in a 3-1 win at the Nou Camp. His first goal, a **chip over the keeper**, is a **Champions League** classic.

SEMI-FINAL FIRST LEG VS REAL MADRID, 2011

Messi scored **both goals** in a 2-0 win at the Bernabéu. His second—a **dazzling solo run** through Madrid's defense—became one of his most career-defining goals.

SEMI-FINAL FIRST LEG VS. BAYERN MUNICH, 2015

Messi's **second goal** saw him **dribble past** Jérôme Boateng before producing a **famous chip** over keeper Manuel Neuer. Pep Guardiola was Bayern boss too!

QUARTER-FINAL SECOND LEG VS. ARSENAL, 2010

Messi scored all **four goals** in a 4-1 win at the Nou Camp, including a **thunderous strike** into the top corner. One of the most **dominant individual displays** the competition has ever seen.

QUARTER-FINAL SECOND LEG VS. PSG, 2013

With Barcelona needing a spark, Messi **came off the bench** while injured and immediately changed the game. His **run and assist** helped turn the tie, sending Barca through on away goals.

BARCELONA

HONORS AND STATS

Leo Messi's major honors, awards, and statistics from his unmatched Barcelona career.

COPA DEL REY

2008-09
2011-12
2014-15
2015-16
2016-17
2017-18
2020-21

CHAMPIONS LEAGUE

2005-06
2008-09
2010-11
2014-15

LA LIGA

2004-05
2005-06
2008-09
2009-10
2010-11
2012-13
2014-15
2015-16
2017-18
2018-19

FIFA CLUB WORLD CUP

2009
2011
2015

SUPERCOPA DE ESPAÑA

2006
2009
2010
2011
2013
2016
2018

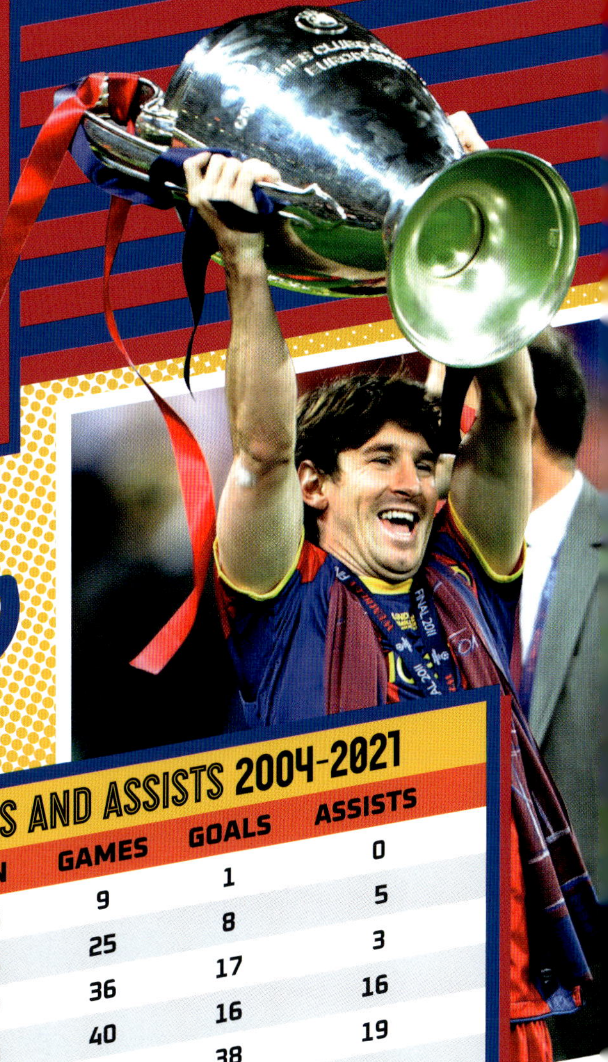

BALLON D'OR

2009
2010
2011
2012
2015
2019
2021

LA LIGA BEST PLAYER

2008-09
2009-10
2010-11
2011-12
2012-13
2014-15

CHAMPIONS LEAGUE TOP SCORER

2008-09
2009-10
2010-11
2011-12
2014-15
2018-19

GOALS AND ASSISTS 2004-2021

SEASON	GAMES	GOALS	ASSISTS
2004-05	9	1	0
2005-06	25	8	5
2006-07	36	17	3
2007-08	40	16	16
2008-09	51	38	19
2009-10	53	47	12
2010-11	55	53	27
2011-12	60	73	32
2012-13	50	60	17
2013-14	46	41	14
2014-15	57	58	31
2015-16	49	41	24
2016-17	52	54	20
2017-18	54	45	20
2018-19	50	51	22
2019-20	44	31	27
2020-21	47	38	14

VAN

STAR SHOT

"I'M LUCKY TO BE PART OF A TEAM WHO HELP TO MAKE ME LOOK GOOD."

ARGENTINA'S STAR

Messi is a global soccer star and a national icon in Argentina. It was a long journey to success with his country.

At the **2006 World Cup**, an **18-year-old** Messi scored against Serbia and Montenegro to become the **youngest Argentine** to score at the tournament.

Playing alongside his **close pal Sergio Agüero**, Messi's early international triumph was winning the **gold medal** at the **2008 Olympics** in Beijing.

At the **2014 World Cup**, Messi almost single-handedly carried Argentina all the way to the final. He won the **Golden Ball** as the tournament's best player, but Germany lifted the trophy.

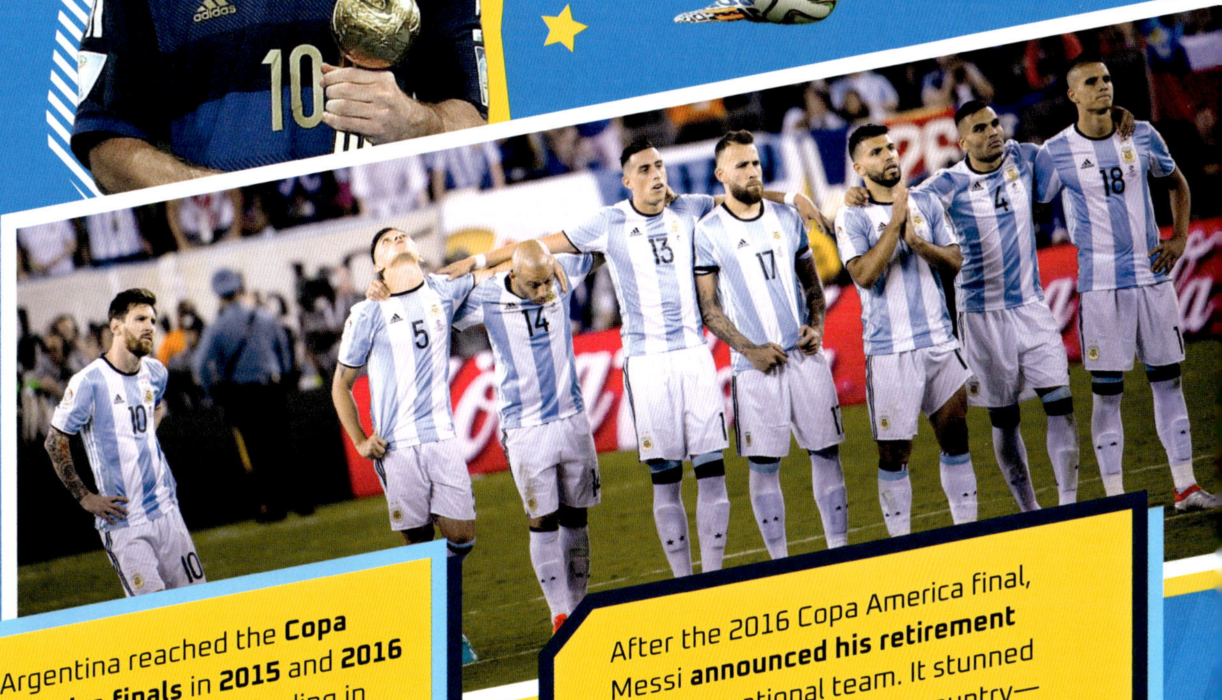

Argentina reached the **Copa America finals** in **2015** and **2016** and Messi was outstanding in both tournaments. But both finals ended in heartbreak against Chile, each **decided by penalties**.

After the 2016 Copa America final, Messi **announced his retirement** from the national team. It stunned Argentina and the whole country—even the president—**urged him to change his mind**. Thankfully, he did, and success followed.

PARIS CALLING

In 2021, after more than two decades at Barcelona, Messi moved to Paris Saint-Germain on a free transfer that shocked the soccer world. And his excellence continued.

1

Messi was **reunited with Neymar** and along with superstar striker **Kylian Mbappé**, he helped PSG **dominate** French soccer and shine in Europe.

2

He helped PSG win **back-to-back Ligue 1 titles** in 2021-22 and 2022-23.

3

In 2022-23, Messi finished with **16 league assists**, the highest in Ligue 1 that season.

4

In two seasons at PSG, he scored **32 goals** and provided **35 assists** in **75 games**, becoming one of the team's most creative forces.

5

While at PSG, he became the first player in history to pass more than **1,000 club career goal contributions** (goals and assists).

6

Messi won the **Trophée des Champions** in 2022, scoring in the final against Nantes.

PSG HONORS AND STATS

LIGUE 1
2021-22
2022-23

TROPHÉE DE CHAMPIONS
2022

GOALS AND ASSISTS 2021 - 2023

SEASON	GAMES	GOALS	ASSISTS
2021-22	34	11	15
2022-23	41	21	20

STAR SHOT

"I HAVE FUN LIKE A CHILD IN THE STREET. WHEN THE DAY COMES WHEN I'M NOT ENJOYING IT, I WILL LEAVE FOOTBALL."

BACK FOR HIS COUNTRY

Messi came out of retirement to lead Argentina through qualifying for the 2018 World Cup in Russia.

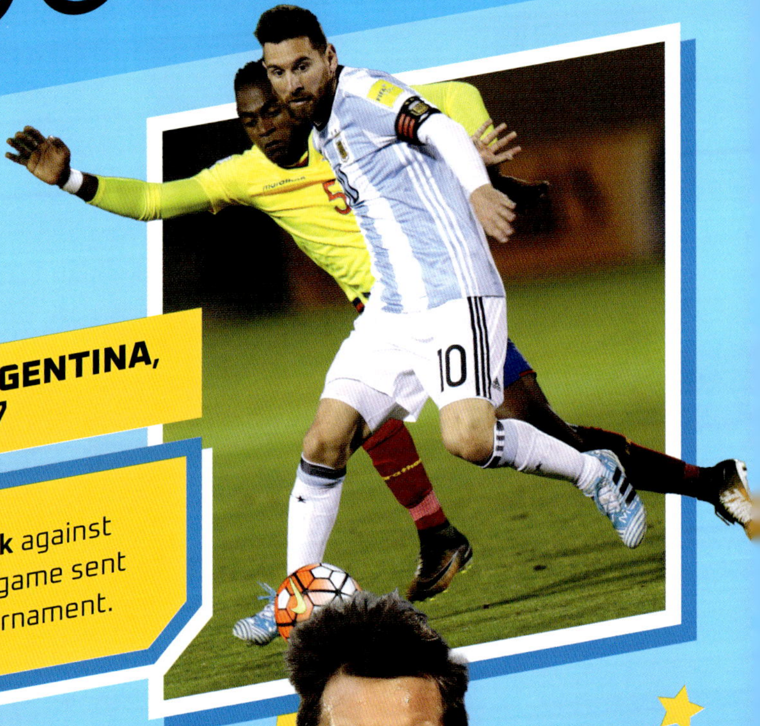

ECUADOR 1 - 3 ARGENTINA, OCTOBER 11, 2017

His **brilliant hat-trick** against Ecuador in the final game sent Argentina to the tournament.

NIGERIA 1 - 2 ARGENTINA, JUNE 26, 2018

In Russia, Messi scored a **stunning goal** against Nigeria, controlling the ball with **two perfect touches** before **firing** into the corner.

FRANCE 4 - 3 ARGENTINA, JUNE 30, 2018

Messi **set up two goals** in a **thrilling 4-3 game**, but the young Mbappé's pace and power proved decisive. Another painful exit, and the wait for a trophy continued.

COPA CHAMPION

In Brazil, Messi scored goals, created chances, and inspired the team with his leadership.

BRAZIL 0 - 1 ARGENTINA, JULY 11, 2021

Argentina beat Brazil 1-0 in the final at the Maracanã to win their first major trophy in 28 years. Messi was named **Player of the Tournament**. It was a defining moment for his international career.

WORLD CHAMPION

At the 2022 World Cup in Qatar, Lionel Messi delivered a career-defining performance to finally lead Argentina to glory.

ARGENTINA 1 - 2 SAUDI ARABIA, NOVEMBER 22, 2022

Argentina's World Cup began with a **shock**. Messi opened the scoring from the penalty spot, but Saudi Arabia stunned the tournament with **two second half goals**. Every game after that became a must win.

ARGENTINA 3 - 0 CROATIA, DECEMBER 13, 2022

Messi led his country to the semi-final, where he produced one of **his greatest World Cup performances**. He opened the scoring from the penalty spot, then delivered an **incredible run** to set up Julián Álvarez for Argentina's third.

ARGENTINA 3 - 3 FRANCE (4–2 PENS), DECEMBER 18, 2022

Messi scored once from the **penalty spot** and once in extra time as Argentina and Kylian Mbappé's France played a **thrilling, all-time classic final** that ended 3-3. Messi scored in the shootout as Argentina **triumphed 4-2** on penalties.

At last, **he lifted the World Cup trophy**—the crowning achievement of his career.

MESSI IN MIAMI FAST FACTS

In 2023, Messi took on a new challenge and moved to the USA to Major League Soccer (MLS) side, Inter Miami. Here are five fast facts about his move that transformed the MLS and led to "Messimania."

1

A month after joining the club, Messi **captained** Miami to their first-ever trophy, the **2023 Leagues Cup**, scoring **10 goals** in seven tournament games.

2

He won the **Ballon d'Or** for the **eighth** time and became the first soccer to be named **Time Magazine**'s Athlete of the Year.

3

Messi ended the 2024 regular season with **20 goals**, bringing his total to **34** to become Inter Miami's **all-time top scorer**.

4

During the 2025 season, he **reached 40 goal contributions faster** than any player in MLS history.

5

During the 2025 MLS Cup play-offs, Messi hit a total of **405 career assists**—breaking the 60-year record held by Ferenc Puskás.

THREE OF THE BEST

Check out Messi's top three performances in the iconic pink strip of Inter Miami.

NASHVILLE SC 1 - **1 INTER MIAMI** (10-11 PENS) LEAGUES CUP FINAL, AUGUST 19, 2023

Messi opened the scoring with a **brilliant solo strike** and later converted in the shootout, leading Miami to the **first trophy** in club history and earning tournament **MVP** (Most Valuable Player) honours.

INTER MIAMI 6 - 2 NEW ENGLAND REVOLUTION, OCTOBER 19, 2024

On the final day of the regular season, Messi scored his **first Inter Miami hat-trick**, helping the club secure a league record 74 points.

INTER MIAMI 3
VANCOUVER WHITECAPS 1
MLS CUP FINAL,
DECEMBER 6, 2025

In the biggest game in club history, Messi delivered **two assists**, guiding Miami to their first **MLS Cup**, and was named **MLS Cup MVP**.

INTER MIAMI HONORS AND STATS

MLS CUP	SUPPORTERS' SHIELD	LEAGUES CUP
2025	2024	2023

GOALS AND ASSISTS 2022-2025

SEASON	GAMES	GOALS	ASSISTS
2022	14	11	5
2023	25	23	13
2024	49	43	26

ARE YOU A MESSI SUPERFAN?

Here are seven signs that you are!

1 You know Messi's stats for every era of his career and can list his trophies without pausing for breath.

2 You've watched every Messi documentary, interview, and behind-the-scenes clip, from his La Masia days to World Cup glory.

3 Whenever soccer comes up in conversation, you somehow find a way to mention Messi's dribbles, goals, assists, or records.

4

When playing soccer with friends, you always try to copy Messi's left foot curlers, close control, and impossible passes.

5

You follow multiple Messi fan pages, so you're always first to know about his milestones, awards, and magical moments.

6

Your wardrobe includes at least one Barcelona, Argentina, PSG, or Inter Miami number 10 shirt—maybe even all four.

7

Watching Messi lift trophies, break records, and create moments of pure genius is your ultimate football joy.

TEST YOUR KNOWLEDGE OF THE SOCCER SUPERSTAR ON PAGE 66.

STAR SHOT

"YOU HAVE TO SHOW UP IN THE WORLD CUP, AND IN THE WORLD CUP ANYTHING CAN HAPPEN."

AFA
10
10

ULTIMATE MESSI QUIZ

Take the ultimate Messi quiz to test your knowledge. Score one goal for each correct answer.

1 **With which club did Lionel Messi begin his professional career?**

- **A.** Newell's Old Boys ☐
- **B.** Barcelona ☐
- **C.** Espanyol ☐

2 **Which shirt number is Messi most famous for?**

- **A.** 8 ☐
- **B.** 9 ☐
- **C.** 10 ☐

3 **How many Ballon d'Or awards has Messi won?**

- **A.** Six ☐
- **B.** Seven ☐
- **C.** Eight ☐

4 **Which trophy did Messi win first with Inter Miami?**

- **A.** MLS Cup ☐
- **B.** Leagues Cup ☐
- **C.** Supporters' Shield ☐

5 Which record did Messi break in 2024 with Inter Miami?

A. Most assists in a single MLS game ☐
B. Most hat-tricks in MLS history ☐
C. Fastest goal in MLS history ☐

6 Whose all-time assist record did Messi beat in 2025?

A. Pelé ☐
B. Ferenc Puskás ☐
C. Xavi ☐

7 Which major international trophy did Messi win in 2022?

A. Copa América ☐
B. World Cup ☐
C. Confederations Cup ☐

8 Which club did Messi join after leaving Barcelona in 2021?

A. Manchester City ☐
B. PSG ☐
C. Inter Milan ☐

Check out your answers on page 72, then put a tick in a goal for each question you got right.

MESSI THE RECORD BREAKER

As one of the greatest soccer players of all time, Lionel Messi is a multiple record breaker. Here are 20 of the most significant...

- ★ Most Ballon d'Or Awards – **8**
- ★ Most goals scored for a single club – **672** (for Barcelona)
- ★ Most goals scored in a domestic league – **474**, (for Barcelona)
- ★ Most European Golden Shoe Awards – **6**
- ★ Most goals scored in a calendar year – **91** (2012)
- ★ Most hat-tricks in the Champions League – **8** (level with Cristiano Ronaldo)
- ★ Most assists in soccer history – **405+** (across all competitions)
- ★ Most goals for Argentina – **100+**
- ★ Most appearances for Argentina – **200+ caps**
- ★ Most goals in a single European season – **73** (2011-12)

- Most times La Liga top scorer – **8**
- Most La Liga titles won by a foreign player – **10**
- Most assists in La Liga history – **192**
- Most goals in El Clásico – **26**
- Most trophies won with Barcelona – **34**
- Most man of the match awards at the World Cup – **11**
- Most goals scored in a single Champions League match – **5**
- Only player to win the Ballon d'Or while playing club soccer in both Europe and North America
- Most assists in a single MLS game – **5** (for Inter Miami, 2024)
- First player to win back-to-back MLS MVP awards (2024 and 2025)

ANSWERS

ULTIMATE MESSI QUIZ

1. B - Barcelona

2. C - 10

3. C - Eight

4. B - Leagues Cup

5. A - Most assists in a single MLS game

6. B - Ferenc Puskás

7. B - World Cup

8. B - PSG

PICTURE CREDITS

The publishers would like to thank the following sources for their kind permission to reproduce the pictures in this book.

ALAMY: 360b 30L; Gill Allen/AP 16BL; Allstar Picture Library Ltd 29T, 48BL; Alter Photos/Sipa US 41L; Hassan Ammar/AP 24B; Archivio GBB 10R; Chris Arjoon/Icon Sportswire 68; Bernat Armangue/AP 13BL; Christian Bertrand 44BR; Giuliano Bevilacqua/Abaca Press 36; Rebecca Blackwell/AP 31TL; Bagu Blanco/Aflo Sport 44BC; Luca Bruno/AP 25T; Chris Brunskill/UPI 56L; Byagosmuniz 18; Peter Byrne/PA 17R; Catennaccio 57BL; Daniel Chesterton/PHC Images 54BR; Felipe Dana/AP 49T; Diebilderwelt 56BR; Meng Dingbo/Xinhua 63; dpa picture alliance 37, 39TL, 55TL; Matt Dunham/AP 20-21; Darryl Dyck/The Canadian Press 61T; Fabideciria 64-65; Manu Fernandez/AP 25B, 27TR, 27L, 27BR, 28TR, 38R, 39R, 41BR, 42R, 45, 66; Burt Granofsky/Cal Sport Media 19T; Lionel Hahn/Abaca Press 48R; Hindustan Times/Imago 19BL; HMB Media 61BL; Gao Jing/Xinhua 58B; David Klein/Sportimage 57TR, 59T; Kevin Kolczynski/AP 8; Igor Kralj/Pixsell 1; Andres Kudacki/AP 24T, 40BL, 41TR, 69BL; Laurent Lairys/DPPI 55R, 55BL; Israel Leal/AP 33R; Christian Liewig/Abaca Press 28B; Cristian Martin 31R; Ricardo Mazalan/AP 7; Martin Meissner/AP 49L; Matthieu Mirville/DPPI 51; Joan Monfort/AP 14-15; Emilio Morenatti/AP 43TR; Karel Navarro/AP 32R; Dolores Ochoa/AP 54R; Daniel Ochoa de Olza/AP 39BL; Matias J. Ocner/Miami Herald/Zuma Press 58C, 59BL; Andre Paes 57BR; Alejandro Pagni 5; Natallia Pershaj 35L; Jordan Pettitt/PA 17L; Powerpics 11TL; Diego Radames/SOPA Images/Sipa USA 31B; Raj Valley 19BR; David Ramos/AP 38BL, 43L, 46-47; Martin Rickett/PA 62; Andrew Rowland 50; JC Ruiz/Sipa US 16C; Kevin Schultz/CSM/Zuma Press 23B, 59BR; Lynne Sladky/AP 60BL; Mark Smith/Zuma Press 49B; Nick Tre. Smith/Icon Sportswire 60R; Pierre Tremoussa/Abaca Press 26; Michael Weber/imageBroker 52-53; Jonathan Weiss 35BR; Seth Wenig/AP 67; WireStock 34R; Martin Zabala/Xinhua 9, 69BR; Zuma Press 11R

GETTY IMAGES: Marcelo Boeri/El Grafico 13TL, 13TR; Alex Caparros 35TR; Denis Doyle 22, 23R; Lluis Gene/AFP 23L, 29B; Laurence Griffiths 40R; Jasper Juinen 42BL; John Keeble 34BL; Josep Lago/AFP 32BL; Christian Liewig/Corbis 43BL; Hugo Ortuno 33TL; Visionhaus 30R

OFFSIDE SPORTS PHOTOGRAPHY: L'Equipe 11BR, 12; MarcaMedia 10L

SHUTTERSTOCK: Agencia Efe 33B